PUBLISHED BY NICHOLAS THOMPSON

Woman and Fitness: Female Body

Recomposition, Workout and Diet

@ Leon Laird

Published By Nicholas Thompson

@ Leon Laird

Woman and Fitness: Female Body

Recomposition, Workout and Diet

All Right RESERVED

ISBN 978-87-975096-0-9

TABLE OF **CONTENTS**

Grilled Salmon With Steamed Broccoli And Quinoa: 1

Spinach And Feta Stuffed Chicken Breast With Roasted Sweet Potatoes: 3

Mediterranean Lentil Salad 5

Butternut Squash And Chickpea Curry 7

Mediterranean Vegetable Stir Fry 9

Roasted Red Pepper And Feta Dip 11

Smoked Salmon And Avocado Toast 13

Rice Cakes With Nut Butter And Banana Slices 15

Apple Slices With Almond Butter 16

Edam Me Salad 17

Quinoa Bowl With Roasted Vegetables 19

Zucchini Fritters With Poached Eggs 20

Greek Salad With Grilled Chicken 23

Baked Salmon With Roasted Vegetables 24

Veggie Stir-Fry With Tofu 27

Baked Cod With Lemon-Herb Quinoa 30

Rainbow Garden Delight Platter 34

Mediterranean Herb Medley Platter............................... 36

Baked Tofu With Stir-Fried Vegetables And Brown Rice: 38

Greek Salad With Grilled Shrimp And Whole Grain Pita Bread: 41

Roasted Veggie And Hummus Wrap 44

Chickpea And Spinach Salad.. 46

Lentil Soup With Mediterranean Spices.......................... 48

Baked Salmon With Roasted Asparagus: 50

Turkey Chili With Mixed Beans And Vegetables: 52

Stir-Fried Tofu With Broccoli And Bell Peppers:.............. 55

Grilled Halloumi With Watermelon And Mint 57

Mediterranean Bruschetta... 59

Lemon-Oregano Grilled Chicken 61

Chocolate Avocado Pudding 63

Yogurt Parfait With Granola And Berries 65

Coconut Chia Seed Pudding 66

Grilled Steak With Roasted Potatoes 68

Avocado And Tomato Salad 70

Roasted Brussels Sprouts With Bacon............................ 72

Lemon Herb Chicken With Roasted Brussels Sprouts 74

Shrimp And Broccoli Stir-Fry 76

Baked Eggplant Parmesan 79

Avocado And Tomato Bruschetta 80

Roasted Chickpeas 83

Southwestern Fiesta Platter.. 85

Baked Cinnamon Apple Chips 87

Chia Berry Parfait 89

Turkey And Vegetable Wrap With Hummus And Sliced Bell Peppers.. 91

Roasted Vegetable And Chickpea Bowl With A Drizzle Of Tahini Dressing 93

Beef Stir-Fry With Broccoli, Bell Peppers, And Brown Rice:... 95

Greek Salad With Quinoa 98

Mediterranean Veggie Wrap... 100

- Mediterranean Quinoa Bowl 102
- Balsamic Roasted Chicken Thighs 104
- Chicken And Vegetable Skewers 106
- Chicken And Spinach Stuffed Portobello Mushrooms . 107
- Banana Nice Cream 109
- Blueberry Oatmeal Muffins 111
- Almond Butter Energy Balls 113
- Grilled Vegetable Skewers 115
- Baked Sweet Potato Fries 117
- Spicy Black Bean Burgers 119
- Mediterranean Stuffed Pita Pockets 121
- Mediterranean Stuffed Bell Peppers 123
- Greek Lemon Chicken 125
- Chicken Souvlaki 127
- Chicken And Artichoke Stew 128
- Greek Yogurt Veggie Dip 131
- Coconut Flour Banana Bread 135
- Avocado Chocolate Mousse 136

Grilled Salmon With Steamed Broccoli And Quinoa:

Ingredients:

- 1 cup broccoli florets
- 1/2 cup cooked quinoa
- 1 salmon fillet
- Salt and pepper to taste

Directions:

1. Preheat the grill to medium-high heat.
2. Season the salmon fillet with salt and pepper.
3. Grill the salmon for about 4-5 minutes per side, or until cooked to your desired doneness.
4. Meanwhile, steam the broccoli florets until tender.

5. Serve the grilled salmon with steamed broccoli and a side of cooked quinoa.

Spinach And Feta Stuffed Chicken Breast With Roasted Sweet Potatoes:

Ingredients:

- 1 cup fresh spinach leaves
- 1/4 cup crumbled feta cheese
- 1 large sweet potato, peeled and diced
- 1 tablespoon olive oil
- 2 boneless, skinless chicken breasts
- Salt and pepper to taste
- 1/2 teaspoon dried thyme

Directions:

1. Preheat the oven to 400°F (200°C).

2. Season the chicken breasts with salt and pepper.
3. Make a slit in the side of each chicken breast to create a pocket.
4. Stuff each chicken breast with spinach leaves and crumbled feta cheese.
5. Place the stuffed chicken breasts on a baking sheet lined with parchment paper.
6. Toss the diced sweet potatoes with olive oil, dried thyme, salt, and pepper.
7. Spread the sweet potatoes on the same baking sheet.
8. Bake in the preheated oven for about 25-30 minutes, or until the chicken is cooked through and the sweet potatoes are tender.
9. Serve the stuffed chicken breast with roasted sweet potatoes.

Mediterranean Lentil Salad

Ingredients:

- 1 cup of cherry tomatoes, halved
- 1/2 cup of crumbled feta cheese
- 2 tablespoons of olive oil
- 1 tablespoon of lemon juice
- Salt and pepper to taste
- 1 cup of cooked green lentils
- 1 cup of chopped cucumber
- Fresh herbs for garnish (parsley, mint)

Directions:

1. In a large bowl, combine the lentils, cucumber, tomatoes, and feta cheese.
2. Drizzle olive oil and lemon juice over the mixture.
3. Season with salt and pepper and toss well to combine.
4. Garnish with fresh herbs before serving.

Butternut Squash And Chickpea Curry

Ingredients:

- 2 cloves of garlic, minced

- 1 can of coconut milk

- 1 tablespoon of curry powder

- 1 tablespoon of olive oil

- Salt and pepper to taste

- Fresh coriander for garnish

- 2 cups of cubed butternut squash

- 1 can of chickpeas, drained and rinsed

- 1 onion, chopped

Directions:

1. In a large pot, heat the olive oil and sauté the onion and garlic until translucent.
2. Add the curry powder and cook for another minute.
3. Add the butternut squash, chickpeas, and coconut milk to the pot. Bring to a simmer.
4. Cover the pot and let it cook for about 30 minutes, or until the squash is tender.
5. Season with salt and pepper. Garnish with fresh coriander before serving.

Mediterranean Vegetable Stir Fry

Ingredients:

- 1 clove of garlic, minced
- 1 teaspoon of dried herbs (basil, oregano, rosemary)
- Salt and pepper to taste
- 2 cups of assorted Mediterranean vegetables (bell peppers, zucchini, eggplant), sliced
- 1 tablespoon of olive oil
- Fresh herbs for garnish

Directions:

1. Heat the olive oil in a large skillet or wok over medium heat.
2. Add the garlic and sauté until fragrant.

3. Add the sliced vegetables to the skillet. Stir fry for about 10-15 minutes, or until the vegetables are tender.
4. Season with dried herbs, salt, and pepper. Garnish with fresh herbs before serving.

Roasted Red Pepper And Feta Dip

Ingredients:

- 1 garlic clove, minced
- 1 tablespoon of lemon juice
- 1 tablespoon chopped fresh parsley
- Salt and pepper to taste
- 2 roasted red peppers, chopped
- 4 ounces feta cheese
- 1/4 cup Greek yogurt
- Pita bread or veggies for serving

Directions:

1. Preheat oven to 400°F.

2. In a food processor, combine the roasted red peppers, feta cheese, Greek yogurt, garlic, lemon juice, parsley, salt, and pepper.
3. Process until smooth and creamy.
4. Transfer the dip to a small baking dish.
5. Bake for 15-20 minutes or until the dip is slightly browned on top.
6. Serve hot with pita bread or veggies.

Smoked Salmon And Avocado Toast

Ingredients:

- 1 avocado, mashed
- 4 ounces smoked salmon
- 1 tablespoon chopped fresh dill
- 4 slices whole grain bread, toasted
- Salt and pepper to taste

Directions:

1. Spread the mashed avocado evenly on the toasted bread slices.
2. Top each toast with smoked salmon.
3. Sprinkle the chopped dill, salt, and pepper on top.
4. Serve immediately.

Rice Cakes With Nut Butter And Banana Slices

Ingredients:

- Rice cakes

- Nut butter (such as almond butter or peanut butter)

- Banana, sliced

Directions:

1. Spread nut butter on top of each rice cake.
2. Place banana slices on top of the nut butter.
3. Serve the rice cakes with nut butter and banana slices.

Apple Slices With Almond Butter

Ingredients:

- Apple, sliced

- Almond butter

Directions:

1. Slice the apple into thin wedges or rounds.
2. Spread almond butter on top of each apple slice.
3. Serve the apple slices with almond butter as a satisfying and fiber-rich snack.

Edam Me Salad

Ingredients:

- Diced red onion

- Chopped fresh parsley or cilantro

- Olive oil

- Lemon juice

- Cooked edamame beans

- Diced cucumber

- Diced red bell pepper

- Salt and pepper to taste

Directions:

1. In a bowl, combine the cooked edam me beans, diced cucumber, diced red bell pepper, diced red onion, and chopped fresh parsley or cilantro.
2. Drizzle with olive oil and lemon juice.
3. Add salt and pepper, then blend by tossing.
4. Serve the edam me salad as a protein-packed and refreshing snack or side dish.

Quinoa Bowl With Roasted Vegetables

Ingredients:

- 1 teaspoon dried oregano
- 1 teaspoon dried thyme
- Salt and freshly ground black pepper
- 1 red bell pepper, chopped
- 1 yellow bell pepper, chopped
- 1 zucchini, chopped
- 1 cup uncooked quinoa
- 2 tablespoons olive oil
- 2 teaspoons garlic powder
- 1 red onion, chopped

Directions:

1. Preheat oven to 400°F.
2. Cook quinoa according to package directions.
3. Meanwhile, in a large bowl, combine olive oil, garlic powder, oregano, thyme, salt, and pepper. Add bell peppers, zucchini, and onion and toss to coat.
4. Spread vegetables on a large rimmed baking sheet. Roast in preheated oven for 20 minutes, or until vegetables are tender.
5. Serve quinoa topped with roasted vegetables.

Zucchini Fritters With Poached Eggs

Ingredients:

- 2 tablespoons chopped fresh parsley

- 1 teaspoon garlic powder

- Salt and freshly ground black pepper

- 2 tablespoons olive oil

- 4 large eggs

- 2 cups grated zucchini

- 1/2 cup grated Parmesan cheese

- 1/4 cup all-purpose flour

Directions:

1. In a large bowl, combine zucchini, Parmesan cheese, flour, parsley, garlic powder, salt, and pepper. Mix until combined.
2. Heat oil in a large skillet over medium heat. Form zucchini mixture into 4 patties and add to hot skillet. Cook for 4 minutes per side, or until golden brown.
3. Meanwhile, bring a medium pot of water to a simmer. Crack eggs into simmering water and poach until whites are set and yolks are still runny, about 3 minutes.

4. Serve zucchini fritters topped with poached eggs.

Greek Salad With Grilled Chicken

Ingredients:

- Salt and freshly ground black pepper
- 2 large tomatoes, chopped
- 1 cucumber, diced
- 1/2 red onion, thinly sliced
- 1/2 cup pitted Kalamata olives
- 1/4 cup crumbled feta cheese
- 2 boneless, skinless chicken breasts
- 2 tablespoons olive oil
- 1 teaspoon dried oregano
- 2 tablespoons red wine vinegar

Directions:

1. Heat grill to medium-high heat.
2. Brush chicken with olive oil and season with oregano, salt, and pepper. Grill chicken for 4 to 6 minutes per side, or until cooked through.
3. In a large bowl, combine tomatoes, cucumber, red onion, olives, feta, and red wine vinegar. Toss to combine.
4. Slice chicken and add to salad. Serve.

Baked Salmon With Roasted Vegetables

Ingredients:

- 2 tablespoons olive oil

- 1 teaspoon dried dill

- Salt and pepper to taste

- 2 salmon fillets (6 ounces each)

- 2 cups mixed vegetables (such as broccoli, bell peppers, and zucchini), chopped

- Lemon wedges for serving

Directions:

1. Preheat the oven to 400°F (200°C).
2. Place the salmon fillets on a baking sheet lined with parchment paper.
3. In a bowl, toss the mixed vegetables with olive oil, dried dill, salt, and pepper.
4. Spread the vegetables around the salmon on the baking sheet.
5. Bake for 15-20 minutes or until the salmon is cooked through and the vegetables are tender.
6. Serve with lemon wedges.

Veggie Stir-Fry With Tofu

Ingredients:

- 1 tablespoon sesame oil

- 1 tablespoon olive oil

- 1 clove garlic, minced

- 1/2 teaspoon grated ginger

- Salt and pepper to taste

- 8 ounces extra-firm tofu, drained and cubed

- 2 cups mixed vegetables (such as bell peppers, broccoli, snap peas, and carrots), sliced

- 2 tablespoons low-sodium soy sauce

- Sesame seeds for garnish (optional)

Directions:

1. Heat olive oil in a large skillet or wok over medium heat.
2. Add minced garlic and grated ginger to the skillet. Sauté for 1-2 minutes until fragrant.
3. Add tofu cubes to the skillet and cook until lightly browned on all sides.
4. Push the tofu to one side of the skillet and add the mixed vegetables to the other side. Cook for 3-4 minutes until the vegetables are tender-crisp.
5. In a small bowl, whisk together low-sodium soy sauce and sesame oil.
6. Pour the sauce mixture over the tofu and vegetables in the skillet.
7. Stir to coat everything evenly and cook for another 1-2 minutes until heated through.
8. Season with salt and pepper to taste. Garnish with sesame seeds if desired.
9. Serve hot.

Baked Cod With Lemon-Herb Quinoa

Ingredients:

- 1 lemon, juiced and zested
- 2 tablespoons chopped fresh herbs (such as parsley, dill, or cilantro)
- 1 tablespoon olive oil
- 2 cod fillets (6 ounces each)
- 1 cup quinoa
- 2 cups vegetable broth
- Salt and pepper to taste

Directions:

1. Preheat the oven to 400°F (200°C).

2. Place the cod fillets on a baking sheet lined with parchment paper.
3. Drizzle olive oil over the cod fillets, then season with salt, pepper, and lemon zest.
4. Bake for 15-20 minutes or until the cod is opaque and flakes easily with a fork.
5. While the cod is baking, rinse the quinoa under cold water.
6. In a saucepan, bring the vegetable broth to a boil.
7. Add the rinsed quinoa to the boiling broth, then reduce the heat to low.
8. Cover the saucepan and simmer for 15-20 minutes until the quinoa is tender and the broth is absorbed.
9. Fluff the quinoa with a fork, then stir in lemon juice and chopped fresh herbs.
10. Serve the baked cod on a bed of lemon-herb quinoa.

Smoky Eggplant and Tahiti Dip

Ingredients:

- 1 tbsp extra virgin olive oil
- 1/2 tsp ground cumin
- 1/2 tsp smoked paprika
- Salt and pepper to taste
- 1 large eggplant
- 2 tbsps tahini
- 1 clove garlic, minced
- 2 tbsps lemon juice
- Chopped fresh parsley for garnish

Directions:

1. Preheat the oven to 400°F (200°C).

2. Pierce the eggplant several times with a fork and place it on a baking sheet. Roast in the oven for 25-30 minutes, or until the skin is charred and the flesh is tender.
3. Remove the eggplant from the oven and let it cool. Once cooled, peel off the skin and chop the flesh.
4. In a food processor, combine the roasted eggplant, tahini, minced garlic, lemon juice, olive oil, ground cumin, smoked paprika, salt, and pepper. Blend until smooth.
5. Transfer the dip to a serving bowl, garnish with chopped fresh parsley, and refrigerate for at least 30 minutes before serving.
6. Serve with cucumber slices, whole grain bread, or as a topping for baked potatoes.

Rainbow Garden Delight Platter

Ingredients:

- 1 cup carrot sticks

- 1 cup radishes, sliced

- 1 cup snap peas

- 1 cup broccoli florets

- 1 cup cauliflower florets

- 1 cup cherry tomatoes, halved

- 1 cup cucumber, sliced

- 1 cup bell peppers (assorted colors), sliced

- 1 cup hummus for dipping

Directions:

1. Arrange the cherry tomatoes, cucumber slices, bell pepper slices, carrot sticks, radishes, snap peas, broccoli florets, and cauliflower florets on a large platter.
2. Place a bowl of hummus in the center of the platter.
3. Serve and enjoy!

Mediterranean Herb Medley Platter

Ingredients:

- 1 cup olives (assorted types)
- 1 cup artichoke hearts
- 1 cup roasted red peppers, sliced
- 1 cup feta cheese, crumbled
- 1 tbsp extra virgin olive oil
- 1 tbsp fresh lemon juice
- 1 tsp dried oregano
- 1 cup cherry tomatoes, halved
- 1 cup cucumber, sliced
- 1 cup bell peppers (assorted colors), sliced

- 1 cup zucchini, sliced

- 1 tsp dried thyme

Directions:

1. Arrange the cherry tomatoes, cucumber slices, bell pepper slices, zucchini slices, olives, artichoke hearts, and roasted red pepper slices on a platter.
2. In a small bowl, whisk together the olive oil, lemon juice, dried oregano, dried thyme, salt, and pepper to make the dressing.
3. Drizzle the dressing over the vegetable platter. Sprinkle crumbled feta cheese on top. Serve and enjoy!

Baked Tofu With Stir-Fried Vegetables And Brown Rice:

Ingredients:

- 1 tablespoon cornstarch

- 1 tablespoon vegetable oil

- 1 bell pepper, sliced

- 1 zucchini, sliced

- 1 carrot, julienned

- 2 garlic cloves, minced

- 1 block of firm tofu, drained and pressed

- 2 tablespoons soy sauce

- 1 tablespoon sesame oil

- 1 tablespoon maple syrup

- Cooked brown rice for serving

Directions:

1. Preheat the oven to 400°F (200°C).
2. Cut the pressed tofu into cubes and place them in a bowl.
3. In a separate bowl, whisk together the soy sauce, sesame oil, maple syrup, and cornstarch to make a marinade.
4. Pour the marinade over the tofu cubes and toss gently to coat.
5. Place the tofu cubes on a baking sheet lined with parchment paper.
6. Bake in the preheated oven for about 25-30 minutes, or until the tofu is crispy and golden.
7. Meanwhile, heat the vegetable oil in a large skillet or wok over medium-high heat.
8. Add the bell pepper, zucchini, carrot, and minced garlic to the skillet and stir-fry for

about 5-7 minutes, or until the vegetables are tender-crisp.
9. Serve the baked tofu with stir-fried vegetables and cooked brown rice.

Greek Salad With Grilled Shrimp And Whole Grain Pita Bread:

Ingredients:

- Mixed salad greens
- Cucumber, sliced
- Cherry tomatoes, halved
- Red onion, thinly sliced
- Kalamata olives
- Feta cheese, crumbled
- Lemon wedges
- 1 pound shrimp, peeled and deveined
- 2 tablespoons olive oil

- 1 teaspoon dried oregano

- Salt and pepper to taste

- Whole grain pita bread

Directions:

1. Preheat the grill to medium-high heat.
2. In a bowl, toss the shrimp with olive oil, dried oregano, salt, and pepper.
3. Thread the seasoned shrimp onto skewers.
4. Grill the shrimp for about 2-3 minutes per side, or until cooked through and slightly charred.
5. In a large bowl, combine the mixed salad greens, cucumber slices, cherry tomatoes, red onion, Kalamata olives, and crumbled feta cheese.
6. Toss the salad with your preferred dressing.
7. Serve the Greek salad with grilled shrimp, lemon wedges, and whole grain pita bread.

Roasted Veggie And Hummus Wrap

Ingredients:

- 1 cup of roasted vegetables (bell peppers, zucchini, eggplant)
- 1/2 cup of hummus
- Fresh greens (spinach, lettuce)
- 2 whole grain wraps
- Salt and pepper to taste

Directions:

1. Lay out the wraps and spread a layer of hummus on each one.
2. Arrange the roasted vegetables and fresh greens on top of the hummus.
3. Season with salt and pepper.

4. Roll up the wraps tightly and cut in half before serving.

Chickpea And Spinach Salad

Ingredients:

- 1/2 cup of cucumber, chopped
- 1/4 cup of red onion, thinly sliced
- 2 tablespoons of olive oil
- 1 tablespoon of lemon juice
- 2 cups of spinach
- 1 cup of cooked chickpeas
- 1 cup of cherry tomatoes, halved
- Salt and pepper to taste

Directions:

1. In a large bowl, combine the spinach, chickpeas, cherry tomatoes, cucumber, and red onion.
2. Drizzle the salad with olive oil and lemon juice, then season with salt and pepper.
3. Toss well to combine all the Ingredients: before serving.

Lentil Soup With Mediterranean Spices

Ingredients:

- 2 celery stalks, diced

- 4 cups of vegetable broth

- 1 teaspoon of ground cumin

- 1 teaspoon of ground coriander

- 1/2 teaspoon of turmeric

- 1 tablespoon of olive oil

- Salt and pepper to taste

- 1 cup of dry lentils

- 1 onion, diced

- 2 carrots, diced

- Fresh herbs for garnish

Directions:

1. Rinse the lentils and set aside.
2. Heat the olive oil in a large pot over medium heat. Add the onion, carrots, and celery, then sauté until softened.
3. Add the cumin, coriander, and turmeric, stirring well to combine.
4. Add the lentils and vegetable broth to the pot. Bring the mixture to a boil, then reduce heat and let it simmer for about 30 minutes, or until the lentils are tender.
5. Season with salt and pepper. Garnish with fresh herbs before serving.

Baked Salmon With Roasted Asparagus:

Ingredients:

- Salt and pepper to taste
- 1 bunch of asparagus
- 4 salmon fillets
- 1 tablespoon of olive oil

Directions:

1. Preheat the oven to 400°F (200°C).
2. Season the salmon fillets with salt and pepper.
3. Place the salmon fillets on a baking sheet lined with parchment paper.
4. Trim the ends of the asparagus and toss them with olive oil, salt, and pepper.

5. Arrange the asparagus around the salmon on the baking sheet.
6. Bake for 12-15 minutes or until the salmon is cooked through and the asparagus is tender.

Turkey Chili With Mixed Beans And Vegetables:

Ingredients:

- 1 can (14 ounces) of diced tomatoes

- 1 can (14 ounces) of kidney beans, drained and rinsed

- 1 can (14 ounces) of black beans, drained and rinsed

- 1 bell pepper, diced

- 1 zucchini, diced

- 2 tablespoons of chili powder

- 1 teaspoon of cumin

- 1 tablespoon of olive oil

- 1 onion, diced

- 2 cloves of garlic, minced

- 1 pound of ground turkey

- Salt and pepper to taste

Directions:

1. Heat olive oil in a large pot or Dutch oven over medium heat.
2. Add onion and garlic, and sauté until softened.
3. Add ground turkey and cook until browned.
4. Add diced tomatoes, kidney beans, black beans, bell pepper, zucchini, chili powder, cumin, salt, and pepper. Stir to combine.
5. Bring the chili to a boil, then reduce the heat to low and simmer for 30 minutes, stirring occasionally.
6. Adjust seasoning if needed and serve hot.

Stir-Fried Tofu With Broccoli And Bell Peppers:

Ingredients:

- 2 cups of broccoli florets

- 1 bell pepper, thinly sliced

- 2 cloves of garlic, minced

- 2 tablespoons of low-sodium soy sauce

- 1 tablespoon of rice vinegar

- 1 teaspoon of honey or maple syrup

- 1 tablespoon of sesame oil

- 14 ounces (400g) of firm tofu, cubed

- Sesame seeds for garnish (optional)

Directions:

1. Heat sesame oil in a large skillet or wok over medium-high heat.
2. Add tofu cubes and stir-fry until lightly browned and crispy.
3. Remove tofu from the skillet and set aside.
4. In the same skillet, add broccoli florets, bell pepper, and minced garlic. Stir-fry for 3-4 minutes or until vegetables are tender-crisp.
5. In a small bowl, whisk together soy sauce, rice vinegar, and honey/maple syrup.
6. Add the tofu back to the skillet and pour the sauce over the tofu and vegetables. Stir-fry for an additional 1-2 minutes until everything is coated and heated through.   Garnish with sesame seeds if desired and serve hot.

Grilled Halloumi With Watermelon And Mint

Ingredients:

- 1/4 cup chopped fresh mint

- 1 tablespoon of olive oil

- 1 tablespoon balsamic vinegar

- 8 ounces halloumi cheese, sliced

- 2 cups cubed watermelon

- Salt and pepper to taste

Directions:

1. Preheat grill or grill pan to medium-high heat.
2. Brush the halloo cheese slices with olive oil.
3. Grill the cheese for 2-3 minutes on each side or until golden brown and slightly crispy.

4. In a medium bowl, combine the cubed watermelon, chopped mint, balsamic vinegar, salt, and pepper.
5. Toss well to combine.
6. Serve the grilled halloumi hot with the watermelon and mint salad.

Mediterranean Bruschetta

Ingredients:

- 1/4 cup crumbled feta cheese
- 1 tablespoon chopped fresh basil
- 1 tablespoon balsamic vinegar
- 1 tablespoon olive oil
- 4 slices whole grain bread, toasted
- 1 cup cherry tomatoes, halved
- Salt and pepper to taste

Directions:

1. In a medium bowl, combine the cherry tomatoes, feta cheese, chopped basil, balsamic vinegar, olive oil, salt, and pepper.

2. Toss well to combine.
3. Spoon the tomato mixture evenly over the toasted bread slices.
4. Serve immediately.

Lemon-Oregano Grilled Chicken

Ingredients:

- 2 tbsp lemon juice
- 2 tbsp chopped fresh oregano
- 2 garlic cloves, minced
- 4 boneless, skinless chicken breasts
- 2 tbsp olive oil
- Salt and pepper, to taste

Directions:

1. In a large bowl, whisk together olive oil, lemon juice, oregano, garlic, salt, and pepper.
2. Add chicken to the bowl and toss to coat.
3. Preheat grill to medium-high heat.

4. Grill chicken for 8-10 minutes on each side, until cooked through.
5. Serve hot with your favorite side dish.

Chocolate Avocado Pudding

Ingredients:

- Maple syrup or honey (optional for sweetness)

- Vanilla extract

- Pinch of salt

- Ripe avocados

- Unsweetened cocoa powder

- Optional toppings: fresh berries, shredded coconut, or chopped nuts

Directions:

1. In a food processor or blender, combine ripe avocados, unsweetened cocoa powder, maple

syrup or honey (if desired), vanilla extract, and a pinch of salt.
2. Blend until smooth and creamy.
3. Transfer the chocolate avocado pudding to serving bowls and refrigerate for at least 30 minutes to chill.
4. Serve the pudding with optional toppings for added flavor and texture.

Yogurt Parfait With Granola And Berries

Ingredients:

- Greek yogurt
- Fresh berries (such as strawberries, blueberries, or raspberries)
- Granola
- Honey or maple syrup (optional for sweetness)

Directions:
1. In a glass or bowl, layer Greek yogurt, fresh berries, and granola.
2. Drizzle with honey or maple syrup, if desired.
3. Repeat the layers until all Ingredients: are used.

Coconut Chia Seed Pudding

Ingredients:

- 2 tablespoons chia seeds
- 1 cup unsweetened coconut milk (or any non-dairy milk)
- Unsweetened shredded coconut
- Optional toppings: fresh fruit, nuts, or a drizzle of honey

Directions:

1. In a bowl, combine chia seeds and coconut milk. Stir well.
2. Cover the bowl and refrigerate for at least 2 hours or overnight to allow the chia seeds to expand and create a pudding-like consistency.

3. Serve the coconut chia seed pudding with a sprinkle of shredded coconut and optional toppings.

Grilled Steak With Roasted Potatoes

Ingredients:

- 1 teaspoon dried oregano
- Salt and freshly ground black pepper
- 2 (6-ounce) sirloin steaks
- 2 tablespoons olive oil
- 1 teaspoon garlic powder
- 1 1/2 pounds potatoes, cut into 1-inch cubes

Directions:

1. Preheat oven to 400°F.
2. Heat grill to medium-high heat.
3. In a small bowl, whisk together olive oil, garlic powder, oregano, salt, and pepper. Brush steaks with olive oil mixture.

4. Grill steaks for 4 to 6 minutes per side, or until cooked to desired doneness.
5. Meanwhile, place potatoes on a large rimmed baking sheet. Drizzle with remaining olive oil mixture and season with salt and pepper. Roast in preheated oven for 20 minutes, or until potatoes are tender.
6. Serve steaks with roasted potatoes.

Avocado And Tomato Salad

Ingredients:

- Salt and freshly ground black pepper
- 2 large tomatoes, chopped
- 1 avocado, diced
- 2 tablespoons chopped fresh parsley
- 2 tablespoons olive oil
- 2 tablespoons red wine vinegar
- 1 teaspoon dried oregano
- 2 tablespoons crumbled feta cheese

Directions:

1. In a small bowl, whisk together olive oil, red wine vinegar, oregano, salt, and pepper.
2. In a large bowl, combine tomatoes, avocado, parsley, and feta cheese. Pour olive oil mixture over top and toss to combine.
3. Serve salad at room temperature.

Roasted Brussels Sprouts With Bacon

Ingredients:

- Salt and freshly ground black pepper
- 1 pound Brussels sprouts, trimmed and halved
- 4 slices bacon, diced
- 2 tablespoons olive oil
- 2 cloves garlic, minced

Directions:

1. Preheat oven to 400°F.
2. In a small bowl, whisk together olive oil, garlic, salt, and pepper.
3. Place Brussels sprouts on a large rimmed baking sheet. Drizzle with olive oil mixture and sprinkle bacon over top.

4. Roast in preheated oven for 20 minutes, or until Brussels sprouts are tender and bacon is crisp.

Lemon Herb Chicken With Roasted Brussels Sprouts

Ingredients:

- 2 cloves garlic, minced

- 1 tablespoon chopped fresh herbs (such as thyme or rosemary)

- Salt and pepper to taste

- 2 cups Brussels sprouts, trimmed and halved

- 2 chicken thighs, bone-in and skin-on

- 1 tablespoon olive oil

- 1 lemon, juiced and zested

- 1 tablespoon balsamic vinegar

Directions:

1. Preheat the oven to 400°F (200°C).
2. Put the chicken thighs on a baking sheet lined with parchment paper.
3. In a small bowl, whisk together olive oil, lemon juice, lemon zest, minced garlic, chopped fresh herbs, salt, and pepper.
4. Drizzle the lemon herb mixture over the chicken thighs, rubbing it into the skin.
5. Arrange the halved Brussels sprouts around the chicken on the baking sheet.
6. Drizzle the Brussels sprouts with balsamic vinegar.
7. Bake for 30-35 minutes or until the chicken is cooked through and the Brussels sprouts are crispy and tender.
8. Serve hot.

Shrimp And Broccoli Stir-Fry

Ingredients:

- 2 tablespoons low-sodium soy sauce

- 1 tablespoon sesame oil

- 1 tablespoon olive oil

- 1 clove garlic, minced

- 1/2 teaspoon grated ginger

- 8 ounces shrimp, peeled and deveined

- 2 cups broccoli florets

- 1 cup sliced bell peppers

- 1/2 cup sliced mushrooms

- Salt and pepper to taste

Directions:

1. Heat olive oil in a skillet or wok over medium heat.
2. **Add minced garlic and grated ginger to the skillet. Sauté for 1-2 minutes until fragrant.**
3. Add shrimp to the skillet and cook until pink and cooked through.
4. Remove the shrimp from the skillet and set aside.
5. In the same skillet, add broccoli florets, sliced bell peppers, and sliced mushrooms.
6. Stir-fry the vegetables for 3-4 minutes until tender-crisp.
7. Return the shrimp to the skillet.
8. Drizzle low-sodium soy sauce and sesame oil over the shrimp and vegetables.
9. Stir to coat everything evenly and cook for another 1-2 minutes until heated through.
10. Season with salt and pepper to taste. Serve hot.

Baked Eggplant Parmesan

Ingredients:

- 1 cup shredded mozzarella cheese
- 1/4 cup grated Parmesan cheese
- 2 tablespoons chopped fresh basil
- 1 tablespoon olive oil
- 1 large eggplant, sliced into rounds
- 1 cup marinara sauce
- Salt and pepper to taste

Directions:

1. Preheat the oven to 375°F (190°C).
2. Place the eggplant slices on a baking sheet lined with parchment paper.

3. Drizzle olive oil over the eggplant slices, then season with salt and pepper.
4. Bake the eggplant slices for 20-25 minutes until tender.
5. Remove the baking sheet from the oven.
6. Spread a thin layer of marinara sauce on each eggplant slice.
7. Sprinkle shredded mozzarella cheese and grated Parmesan cheese on top of the sauce.
8. Return the baking sheet to the oven and bake for another 15-20 minutes until the cheese is melted and bubbly.
9. Remove from the oven and sprinkle chopped fresh basil over the baked eggplant slices. 10. Serve hot.

Avocado And Tomato Bruschetta

Ingredients:

- 1 tomato, diced

- 1 clove garlic, minced

- 1 tablespoon chopped fresh basil

- 1 tablespoon balsamic vinegar

- 4 slices whole grain baguette

- 1 avocado, pitted and mashed

- Salt and pepper to taste

Directions:

1. 2. Preheat the oven to 350°F (175°C).
2. Place the whole grain baguette slices on a baking sheet.
3. Toast the baguette slices in the oven for about 10 minutes or until crispy.
4. In a bowl, combine mashed avocado, diced tomato, minced garlic, chopped fresh basil, balsamic vinegar, salt, and pepper.
5. Mix well until all Ingredients: are combined.

6. Spread the avocado and tomato mixture evenly onto the toasted baguette slices.
7. Serve immediately.

Roasted Chickpeas

Ingredients:

- 1 teaspoon paprika
- 1/2 teaspoon ground cumin
- 1/2 teaspoon garlic powder
- 1/2 teaspoon salt
- 2 cups cooked chickpeas
- 1 tablespoon olive oil
- 1/4 teaspoon cayenne pepper (optional)

Directions:

1. Preheat the oven to 400°F (200°C).
2. Rinse and drain the cooked chickpeas, then pat them dry with a paper towel.

3. In a bowl, combine chickpeas, olive oil, paprika, ground cumin, garlic powder, salt, and cayenne pepper (if desired).
4. Toss the chickpeas until they are evenly coated with the seasoning mixture.
5. Spread the seasoned chickpeas in a single layer on a baking sheet lined with parchment paper.
6. Roast the chickpeas in the oven for 30-35 minutes, stirring once or twice, until they are crispy and golden brown.
7. Remove from the oven and let them cool before serving.

Southwestern Fiesta Platter

Ingredients:

- 1 cup red onion, thinly sliced
- 1 cup avocado, diced
- 1 tbsp lime juice
- 1 tbsp chopped fresh cilantro
- 1 tsp ground cumin
- 1 tsp chili powder
- 1 cup cherry tomatoes, halved
- 1 cup bell peppers (assorted colors), sliced
- 1 cup jicama, julienned
- 1 cup black beans, rinsed and drained

- 1 cup corn kernels

- Salt and pepper to taste

Directions:

1. Arrange the cherry tomatoes, bell pepper slices, jicama, black beans, corn kernels, and red onion on a platter.
2. In a small bowl, combine the diced avocado, lime juice, chopped cilantro, ground cumin, chili powder, salt, and pepper to make the creamy avocado dip.
3. Serve the avocado dip in a separate bowl alongside the vegetable platter. Serve and enjoy!

Baked Cinnamon Apple Chips

Ingredients:

- 2 apples (such as Granny Smith or Honeycrisp), cored and thinly sliced
- 1 tbsp low glycemic index sweetener (such as coconut sugar or erythritol)
- 1 tsp ground cinnamon

Directions:

1. Preheat the oven to 200°F (95°C) and line a baking sheet with parchment paper.
2. In a bowl, toss the thinly sliced apples with low glycemic index sweetener and ground cinnamon until evenly coated.
3. Arrange the apple slices in a single layer on the prepared baking sheet.

4. Bake for 1.5 to 2 hours, or until the apple chips are crispy and lightly browned, flipping them halfway through.
5. Remove from the oven and let them cool completely before serving.

Chia Berry Parfait

Ingredients:

- 1 tbsp low glycemic index sweetener (such as stevia or monk fruit)

- 1 cup mixed berries (such as strawberries, blueberries, and raspberries)

- 2 tbsps chopped nuts (such as almonds or walnuts)

- 4 tbsps chia seeds

- 1 cup unsweetened almond milk

Directions:

1. In a bowl, combine the chia seeds, almond milk, and low glycemic index sweetener. Stir well to ensure the chia seeds are evenly distributed.

2. Cover the bowl and refrigerate for at least 4 hours or overnight, allowing the chia seeds to absorb the liquid and thicken.
3. Once the chia pudding has set, layer it with mixed berries in serving glasses or jars.
4. Top with chopped nuts for added crunch and texture.
5. Serve chilled and enjoy!

Turkey And Vegetable Wrap With Hummus And Sliced Bell Peppers

Ingredients:

- 2 tablespoons hummus

- Sliced bell peppers

- 1 large whole grain tortilla or wrap

- 4 ounces sliced turkey breast

- Mixed greens

Directions:

1. Lay the whole grain tortilla or wrap flat on a clean surface.
2. Spread the hummus evenly on the tortilla or wrap.

3. Layer the sliced turkey breast, sliced bell peppers, and mixed greens on top of the hummus.
4. Roll the tortilla or wrap tightly, folding in the sides as you go.
5. Cut the wrap in half, if desired.
6. Serve and enjoy.

Roasted Vegetable And Chickpea Bowl With A Drizzle Of Tahini Dressing

Ingredients:

- Juice of 1 lemon

- 1 garlic clove, minced

- Water (for thinning the dressing, if needed)

- Assorted vegetables (e.g., sweet potatoes, bell peppers, zucchini, eggplant), chopped

- 1 can chickpeas, rinsed and drained

- 1 tablespoon olive oil

- Salt and pepper to taste

- 1/4 cup tahini

- Cooked quinoa or brown rice for serving

Directions:

1. Preheat the oven to 400°F (200°C).
2. Toss the chopped vegetables and chickpeas with olive oil, salt, and pepper on a baking sheet.
3. Spread them out in a single layer.
4. Roast in the preheated oven for about 25-30 minutes, or until the vegetables are tender and slightly caramelized.
5. Meanwhile, prepare the tahini dressing by whisking together tahini, lemon juice, minced garlic, and a pinch of salt in a small bowl.
6. If the dressing is too thick, add water gradually to achieve the desired consistency.
7. Serve the roasted vegetables and chickpeas over cooked quinoa or brown rice.
8. Drizzle the tahini dressing over the bowl.

Beef Stir-Fry With Broccoli, Bell Peppers, And Brown Rice:

Ingredients:

- 1 tablespoon oyster sauce

- 1 tablespoon cornstarch

- 1 tablespoon vegetable oil

- 2 cloves garlic, minced

- 1/2 head broccoli, cut into florets

- 1 bell pepper, sliced

- 8 ounces beef (such as sirloin or flank steak), thinly sliced

- 2 tablespoons soy sauce

- Cooked brown rice for serving

Directions:

1. In a bowl, combine the thinly sliced beef, soy sauce, oyster sauce, and cornstarch. Toss to coat the beef evenly and set aside.
2. Heat the vegetable oil in a large skillet or wok over high heat.
3. Add the minced garlic to the skillet and stir-fry for about 30 seconds, until fragrant.
4. Add the beef and marinade to the skillet and stir-fry for about 3-4 minutes, or until the beef is browned and cooked through.
5. Remove the beef from the skillet and set aside.
6. In the same skillet, add the broccoli florets and bell pepper slices.
7. Stir-fry for about 3-4 minutes, or until the vegetables are tender-crisp.
8. Return the cooked beef to the skillet and toss to combine with the vegetables.
9. Serve the beef stir-fry over cooked brown rice.

Greek Salad With Quinoa

Ingredients:

- 1/4 cup of Kalamata olives
- 1/4 cup of crumbled feta cheese
- 2 tablespoons of extra virgin olive oil
- 1 tablespoon of lemon juice
- 2 cups of mixed salad greens
- 1 cup of cooked quinoa
- 1 cucumber, diced
- 1 cup of cherry tomatoes, halved
- 1/2 red onion, thinly sliced
- Salt and pepper to taste

Directions:

1. In a large bowl, combine the salad greens, cooked quinoa, cucumber, cherry tomatoes, red onion, Klamath olives, and feta cheese.
2. Drizzle the salad with extra virgin olive oil and lemon juice, then season with salt and pepper.
3. Toss well to combine all the Ingredients: before serving.

Mediterranean Veggie Wrap

Ingredients:

- 1 cup of mixed Mediterranean vegetables (bell peppers, eggplant, zucchini), sliced
- 1/4 cup of sliced red onion
- 1/4 cup of crumbled feta cheese
- 2 whole wheat tortillas or wraps
- 1/2 cup of hummus
- Fresh herbs for garnish (such as parsley or basil)

Directions:

1. Lay out the tortillas or wraps and spread a layer of hummus on each one.

2. Arrange the mixed vegetables and red onion on top of the hummus.
3. Sprinkle with crumbled feta cheese and garnish with fresh herbs.
4. Roll up the wraps tightly and cut in half before serving.

Mediterranean Quinoa Bowl

Ingredients:

- 1/4 cup of Kalamata olives, pitted and sliced
- 1/4 cup of crumbled feta cheese
- 2 tablespoons of extra virgin olive oil
- 1 tablespoon of lemon juice
- Salt and pepper to taste
- 1 cup of cooked quinoa
- 1 cup of mixed Mediterranean vegetables (cherry tomatoes, cucumbers, bell peppers), diced
- Fresh herbs for garnish (such as parsley or basil)

Directions:

1. In a bowl, combine the cooked quinoa, mixed Mediterranean vegetables, Kalamata olives, and crumbled feta cheese.
2. Drizzle the bowl with extra virgin olive oil and lemon juice, then season with salt and pepper.
3. Toss well to combine all the ingredients.
4. Garnish with fresh herbs before serving.

Balsamic Roasted Chicken Thighs

Ingredients:

- 2 tbsp balsamic vinegar
- 1 tbsp honey
- 2 garlic cloves, minced
- 1 tsp dried thyme
- 8 bone-in, skin-on chicken thighs
- 2 tbsp olive oil
- Salt and pepper, to taste

Directions:

1. Preheat oven to 400°F.

2. In a small bowl, whisk together olive oil, balsamic vinegar, honey, garlic, thyme, salt, and pepper.
3. Arrange chicken thighs in a baking dish and brush with the balsamic mixture.
4. Roast chicken in the oven for 30-35 minutes, until cooked through and crispy on the outside.
5. Serve hot with your favorite vegetable side dish.

Chicken And Vegetable Skewers

Ingredients:

- 1 red onion, cut into chunks

- 2 tbsp olive oil

- 2 garlic cloves, minced

- 1 tsp dried oregano

- 1 lb boneless, skinless chicken breast, cut into cubes

- 1 red bell pepper, cut into chunks

- 1 yellow bell pepper, cut into chunks

- 1 zucchini, cut into rounds

- Salt and pepper, to taste

Directions:

1. Preheat grill to medium-high heat.
2. Thread chicken and vegetables onto skewers, alternating between chicken and vegetables.
3. In a small bowl, whisk together olive oil, garlic, oregano, salt, and pepper.
4. Brush the skewers with the olive oil mixture.
5. Grill skewers for 8-10 minutes on each side, until chicken is cooked through and vegetables are tender.
6. Serve hot with a side of quinoa or brown rice.

Chicken And Spinach Stuffed Portobello Mushrooms

Ingredients:

- 2 cups fresh spinach

- 2 garlic cloves, minced

- 1 tsp dried oregano

- Salt and pepper, to taste

- 1/4 cup grated parmesan cheese

- 4 large portobello mushroom caps

- 1 lb ground chicken

- 2 tbsp olive oil

Directions:

1. Preheat oven to 375°F.
2. Remove the stems from the mushrooms and scoop out the gills with a spoon.
3. In a large skillet, heat olive oil over medium-high heat.
4. Add ground chicken, garlic, oregano, salt, and pepper to the skillet and cook until browned, stirring occasionally.

5. Add spinach to the skillet and cook until wilted.
6. Fill each mushroom cap with the chicken-spinach mixture.
7. Sprinkle parmesan cheese over the top of each stuffed mushroom.
8. Bake in the oven for 20-25 minutes, until mushrooms are tender and cheese is melted.
9. Serve hot with a side salad.

Banana Nice Cream

Ingredients:

- Ripe bananas, sliced and frozen
- Optional add-ins: cocoa powder, nut butter, or vanilla extract

Directions:

1. Place the frozen banana slices in a blender or food processor.
2. Blend until smooth and creamy, scraping down the sides as needed.
3. If desired, add cocoa powder, nut butter, or vanilla extract for flavor variations.
4. Blend again until well combined.
5. Transfer the banana nice cream to a bowl and serve immediately.

Blueberry Oatmeal Muffins

Ingredients:

- Cinnamon
- Salt
- Greek yogurt
- Maple syrup
- Eggs
- Vanilla extract
- Rolled oats
- Whole wheat flour
- Baking powder
- Fresh or frozen blueberries

Directions:

1. Preheat the oven to 350°F (175°C) and line a muffin tin with paper liners.
2. In a bowl, combine rolled oats, whole wheat flour, baking powder, cinnamon, and salt.
3. In a separate bowl, whisk together Greek yogurt, maple syrup, eggs, and vanilla extract.
4. Add the wet Ingredients:to the dry Ingredients:and stir until just combined.
5. Gently fold in the blueberries.
6. Divide the batter evenly among the muffin cups.
7. Bake for 20-25 minutes or until a toothpick inserted into the center of a muffin comes out clean.
8. Allow the muffins to cool before serving.

Almond Butter Energy Balls

Ingredients:

- Ground flaxseed

- Honey or maple syrup

- Chia seeds

- Almond butter

- Rolled oats

- Optional add-ins: chopped nuts, dried fruits, or dark chocolate chips

Directions:

1. In a bowl, combine almond butter, rolled oats, ground flaxseed, honey or maple syrup, chia seeds, and any optional add-ins.

2. Stir until well mixed and the Ingredients: are evenly distributed.
3. Shape the mixture into small balls using your hands.
4. Place the energy balls on a baking sheet and refrigerate for at least 30 minutes to firm up.
5. Store the almond butter energy balls in an airtight container in the refrigerator.

Grilled Vegetable Skewers

Ingredients:

- Salt and freshly ground black pepper
- 1 red bell pepper, cut into 1-inch pieces
- 1 yellow bell pepper, cut into 1-inch pieces
- 1 zucchini, cut into 1-inch pieces
- 2 tablespoons olive oil
- 2 cloves garlic, minced
- 2 teaspoons dried oregano
- 1 red onion, cut into 1-inch pieces

Directions:

1. Heat grill to medium-high heat.

2. In a small bowl, whisk together olive oil, garlic, oregano, salt, and pepper.
3. Thread bell peppers, zucchini, red onion onto 8 metal or wooden skewers. Brush with olive oil mixture.
4. Grill skewers for 8 to 10 minutes, turning occasionally, until vegetables are tender.

Baked Sweet Potato Fries

Ingredients:

- 2 tablespoons olive oil
- 1 teaspoon garlic powder
- 1 teaspoon dried oregano
- 2 sweet potatoes, cut into 1/2-inch-thick sticks
- Salt and freshly ground black pepper

Directions:

1. Preheat oven to 425°F.
2. Place sweet potato sticks on a large rimmed baking sheet. Drizzle with olive oil and sprinkle garlic powder, oregano, salt, and pepper over top.

3. Bake in preheated oven for 20 minutes, flipping once halfway through, until sweet potatoes are tender and golden brown.

Spicy Black Bean Burgers

Ingredients:

- 2 cloves garlic, minced

- 1 teaspoon ground cumin

- 1 teaspoon chili powder

- Salt and freshly ground black pepper

- 2 tablespoons olive oil

- 1 (15-ounce) can black beans, drained and rinsed

- 1/2 cup cooked brown rice

- 1/4 cup breadcrumbs

- 2 tablespoons chopped fresh cilantro

Directions:

1. In a large bowl, mash black beans with a fork. Add brown rice, breadcrumbs, cilantro, garlic, cumin, chili powder, salt, and pepper. Mix until combined.
2. Form mixture into 4 patties.
3. Heat oil in a large skillet over medium heat. Add patties and cook for 4 minutes per side, or until golden brown and heated through.

Mediterranean Stuffed Pita Pockets

Ingredients:

- 1/2 cup of hummus
- 1 cup of mixed Mediterranean vegetables (cucumbers, tomatoes, red onions), sliced
- 1/4 cup of crumbled feta cheese
- 2 whole wheat pita pockets
- Fresh herbs for garnish (such as parsley or mint)

Directions:

1. Cut the pita pockets in half to form pockets.
2. Spread a layer of hummus inside each pocket.
3. Stuff the pockets with mixed Mediterranean vegetables.

4. Sprinkle with crumbled feta cheese and garnish with fresh herbs.
5. Serve immediately.

Mediterranean Stuffed Bell Peppers

Ingredients:

- 1 cup of chopped tomatoes
- 1 cup of chopped spinach
- 1/2 cup of crumbled feta cheese
- 1 tablespoon of olive oil
- 4 large bell peppers
- 1 cup of cooked quinoa
- Salt and pepper to taste

Directions:

1. Preheat the oven to 375°F (190°C).
2. Cut off the tops of the bell peppers and remove the seeds and membranes.

3. In a bowl, mix together the cooked quinoa, chopped tomatoes, spinach, feta cheese, olive oil, salt, and pepper.
4. Stuff the bell peppers with the quinoa mixture and place them in a baking dish.
5. Bake for about 30 minutes, or until the peppers are tender and the filling is heated through.
6. Serve hot.

Greek Lemon Chicken

Ingredients:

- 2 tablespoons of olive oil
- 1 teaspoon of dried oregano
- Salt and pepper to taste
- 4 chicken breasts
- Juice of 2 lemons
- 2 cloves of garlic, minced
- Fresh parsley for garnish

Directions:

1. In a bowl, whisk together the lemon juice, minced garlic, olive oil, dried oregano, salt, and pepper.

2. Place the chicken breasts in a baking dish and pour the marinade over them.
3. Let the chicken marinate in the refrigerator for at least 30 minutes.
4. Preheat the oven to 400°F (200°C).
5. Bake the chicken for about 25-30 minutes, or until cooked through.
6. Garnish with fresh parsley before serving.

Chicken Souvlaki

Ingredients:

- 2 garlic cloves, minced
- 1 tsp dried oregano
- Salt and pepper, to taste
- Wooden skewers, soaked in water for 30 minutes
- 1 lb boneless, skinless chicken breast, cut into cubes
- 1/4 cup olive oil
- 2 tbsp lemon juice
- Tzatziki sauce, for serving

Directions:

1. In a large bowl, whisk together olive oil, lemon juice, garlic, oregano, salt, and pepper.
2. Add chicken to the bowl and toss to coat.
3. Cover the bowl and marinate chicken in the fridge for at least 1 hour.
4. Preheat grill to medium-high heat.
5. Thread chicken onto skewers.
6. Grill skewers for 8-10 minutes on each side, until chicken is cooked through and slightly charred.
7. Serve hot with a side of tzatziki sauce.

Chicken And Artichoke Stew

Ingredients:

- 2 tbsp olive oil

- 1 can diced tomatoes

- 2 cups chicken broth

- 1 can artichoke hearts, drained and chopped

- 1 tbsp chopped fresh thyme

- Salt and pepper, to taste

- 1 lb boneless, skinless chicken thighs, cut into bite-sized pieces

- 1 onion, diced

- 3 garlic cloves, minced

- 1/4 cup chopped fresh parsley, for garnish

Directions:

1. In a large pot or Dutch oven, heat olive oil over medium-high heat.
2. Add chicken pieces to the pot and cook until browned on all sides.

3. Remove chicken from the pot and set aside. Add onion and garlic to the pot and cook until softened.
4. Add diced tomatoes and chicken broth to the pot and bring to a simmer.
5. Add chicken, artichoke hearts, thyme, salt, and pepper to the pot and stir to combine.
6. Cover the pot and simmer for 30-40 minutes, until chicken is cooked through and flavors have melded together. Serve hot with a sprinkle of fresh parsley on top.

Greek Yogurt Veggie Dip

Ingredients:

- 1/4 cup chopped green bell pepper
- 1/4 cup chopped red onion
- 1 clove garlic, minced
- 1 tablespoon chopped fresh dill
- 1 tablespoon lemon juice
- 1 cup Greek yogurt
- 1/4 cup chopped cucumber
- 1/4 cup chopped red bell pepper
- Salt and pepper to taste

Directions:

1. In a bowl, combine Greek yogurt, chopped cucumber, chopped red bell pepper, chopped green bell pepper, chopped red onion, minced garlic, chopped fresh dill, lemon juice, salt, and pepper.
2. Mix well until all Ingredients: are thoroughly combined.
3. Taste and adjust the seasonings if needed.
4. Serve the dip with fresh vegetable sticks or whole grain crackers.

Cucumber roll-ups with smoked salmon

Ingredients:

- 1/4 cup whipped cream cheese

- 1 tablespoon chopped fresh dill

- 1 teaspoon lemon juice

- 1 English cucumber

- 4 ounces smoked salmon

- Salt and pepper to taste

Directions:

1. Using a mandolin or a vegetable peeler, slice the cucumber lengthwise into thin strips.
2. In a bowl, combine whipped cream cheese, chopped fresh dill, lemon juice, salt, and pepper.
3. Spread a thin layer of the cream cheese mixture onto each cucumber strip.
4. Place a slice of smoked salmon on top of the cream cheese mixture.
5. Roll up the cucumberstrip tightly, securing it with a toothpick if needed.
6. Repeat the process with the remaining cucumber strips, cream cheese mixture, and smoked salmon.

7. Serve the cucumber roll-ups chilled.

Coconut Flour Banana Bread

Ingredients:

- 1/4 cup coconut oil, melted
- 1/4 cup low glycemic index sweetener (such as coconut sugar or erythritol)
- 1 tsp vanilla extract
- 1/2 cup coconut flour
- 1 tsp baking powder
- 4 ripe bananas, mashed
- 4 eggs
- 1/2 tsp cinnamon
- Pinch of salt

Directions:

1. Preheat the oven to 350°F (175°C) and grease a loaf pan.
2. In a large bowl, combine the mashed bananas, eggs, melted coconut oil, low glycemic index sweetener, and vanilla extract. Mix well.
3. In a separate bowl, whisk together the coconut flour, baking powder, cinnamon, and salt.
4. Gradually add the dry Ingredients: to the wet ingredients, stirring until well combined.
5. Pour the batter into the greased loaf pan and smooth the top.
6. Bake for 45-50 minutes, or until a toothpick inserted into the center comes out clean.
7. Allow the banana bread to cool before slicing and serving.

Avocado Chocolate Mousse

Ingredients:

- 1/4 cup low glycemic index sweetener (such as stevia or xylitol)
- 1/4 cup unsweetened almond milk
- 1 tsp vanilla extract
- Pinch of salt
- 2 ripe avocados
- 1/4 cup unsweetened cocoa powder
- Optional toppings: fresh berries, shaved dark chocolate, or chopped nuts

Directions:

1. In a food processor or blender, combine the avocados, cocoa powder, low glycemic index

sweetener, almond milk, vanilla extract, and salt. Blend until smooth and creamy.
2. Taste and adjust the sweetness if needed by adding more sweetener.
3. Transfer the mixture to serving dishes or glasses and refrigerate for at least 2 hours to chill and firm up.
4. Before serving, garnish with fresh berries, shaved dark chocolate, or chopped nuts if desired.
5. Serve chilled and enjoy!

www.ingramcontent.com/pod-product-compliance
Lightning Source LLC
LaVergne TN
LVHW021239080526
838199LV00088B/4752